Summer in the Arctic

by Isabel Thomas

OXFORD
UNIVERSITY PRESS

What do you think the Arctic is like?

It looks like this for part of the year.

Then some of the frost melts.
It is light for longer.

Little plants come out of the soil.

Now there is a carpet of grass.

Insects feed on plants.
Fish go north for food.

Terns feed on insects and fish.

Terns are in the Arctic all summer.
They have chicks there.

Wood frogs nap in mud.
They wait for the summer.

Then they pop out when the sun appears!

This is an Arctic fox.
It looks like this for part of the year.

It turns darker in summer.
This helps it keep out of sight.

Some animals nap in lairs.
This one comes out in the sun!

The Arctic summer is short.
Lots can happen in a short summer!

has chicks

has a darker coat

pops out of mud

comes out of a lair

Encourage students to match the Arctic animal with what it does in the summer.